I LIKE TO WRITE

Written by
Brian and Anne Moses

Illustrated by
Sharon Davey

CRABTREE
PUBLISHING COMPANY
WWW.CRABTREEBOOKS.COM

First published in Great Britain in 2022 by The Watts Publishing Group
Copyright © The Watts Publishing Group, 2022
First published in Great Britain in 2022 by The Watts Publishing Group
Copyright © The Watts Publishing Group, 2022

Author: Brian and Anne Moses
Series Editor: Melanie Palmer
Series Design: Lisa Peacock
Literacy Consultant: Kate Ruttle
Editorial director: Kathy Middleton
Illustrator: Sharon Davey
Editor: Janine Deschenes
Proofreader: Petrice Custance
Production technician: Margaret Salter
Print coordinator: Katherine Berti

Library and Archives Canada Cataloguing in Publication

CIP Available at the Library of Congress Canada

Library of Congress Cataloging-in-Publication Data

CIP Available at the Library of Congress

Crabtree Publishing Company

www.crabtreebooks.com   1-800-387-7650

Published by Crabtree Publishing Company in 2022.

Printed in the U.S.A./012022/CG20210915

Published in Canada
Crabtree Publishing
616 Welland Ave.
St. Catharines, Ontario
L2M 5V6

Published in the United States
Crabtree Publishing
347 Fifth Ave
Suite 1402-145
New York, NY 10016

I LIKE TO WRITE

Written by
Brian and Anne Moses

Illustrated by
Sharon Davey

CRABTREE
PUBLISHING COMPANY
WWW.CRABTREEBOOKS.COM

Levi, Hannah, William, and Wang Li are learning to write. They each carefully practice their letters.

4

Next, they practice writing their names.

William writes in his workbook.

Hannah writes her name in letters on a rainbow.

Wang Li and Levi write their names on
the class dinosaur mural.

On the weekend, William visits the beach. He writes his name in the sand.

When the weather is cold,
he writes in the snow...

...and on steamy windows.

Hannah arranges the letter magnets into a sentence.

When Hannah's dad is rolling dough, Hannah writes letters with her finger in the flour.

Wang Li helped make a special cake for her brother's birthday.

happy birthday

She writes a happy birthday message with icing.

Sometimes, Levi sends a text message to his dad.
It is a fun way to practice writing.

Levi's dad types a message back. It says, "See you soon!"

When William plays at Levi's house,
they write on the computer.

Hannah and Wang Li like to write notes to each other. They send kind messages and ask questions.

William helps write a shopping list on his dad's tablet.
He types the list as his dad calls out items.

William sometimes adds treats when
his dad isn't looking.

Levi likes to write poems about his dog, Oscar. But when he reads them aloud, Oscar doesn't always pay attention! He finds treats and toys more interesting.

Luckily, Levi doesn't mind. He likes to practice reading his funny rhymes—even if Oscar isn't listening.

William enjoys writing stories, but it isn't always easy to find a quiet place to write. Sometimes he writes in the car, next to his baby sister.

Other times he writes on the floor, behind the sofa.

In the morning, he even writes at the messy breakfast table.

The children like to write stories together in Hannah's treehouse. They work together to think of ideas. Today, they are writing a story about kids who become superheroes.

Sometimes, the children think about what they might write in the future.

They could write facts about life under the ocean.

They could write instructions for how to use a robot.

They could even write a message to astronauts on the Moon!

Writing can be so exciting.

NOTES FOR CAREGIVERS AND EDUCATORS

This book shows children many reasons why writing is fun and important. Children will be inspired to write in many different places and in many different ways, from typing on a keyboard to taking a pencil to paper. Here are some more ideas for how to get the most from this book.

Pages 4-5, 6-7, and 8-9
Ask children to think of places where they have practiced writing letters and their names. Have each child create an acrostic poem with their name. They should write a word that describes them with each letter.

Pages 10-11
Have children practice writing full sentences. Talk about the parts of a sentence, such as ending with a period. Then, invite children to complete the following sentence starters:
My favorite season is ... because ...
Every day, I like to ... because ...
If I lived in ... I would ...

Pages 12-13
Have children write down the date of their birthday on a piece of construction paper. Ask them to decorate the paper with a picture of their favorite birthday cake. Place each child's birthday paper on the wall, in order.

Pages 14-15
Have children practice writing text messages about their days. What important information would they include in these short messages?

Pages 16-17
Invite children to think of their own names for the alien. They might also think of names for the planet that it comes from. Have them write down their ideas.

Pages 18-19
Have children write a kind note to pass to a classmate. Pair them so everyone receives a note.

Pages 20-21
Ask children to write a grocery shopping list with 10 items on it. Invite them to make some other lists of 10, such as 10 kinds of animals, 10 sports teams, or 10 favorite foods.

Pages 22-23 and 24-25
Where do children like to write? Who do they like to share their writing with? Why do they choose these places and people? Encourage them to use adjectives in their answers. If possible, create a writing spot at home or in the classroom, with children's input.

Pages 26-27
Play the snowball writing activity. Each child gets a piece of paper with a story starter. Set a timer for five minutes and let children write a few sentences to start the story. When the timer is up, they will crumple the papers and throw them to the front of the room. Each child picks up a different paper and continues the story. Repeat a few times.

Pages 28-29
Have children complete one of the prompts on page 29. How do the robot instructions differ from the astronaut messages?

BOOKS TO SHARE

Dear Dinosaur
by Chae Strathie, illustrated by Nicola O'Byrne (Scholastic, 2017)

Idea Jar
by Adam Lehrhaupt, illustrated by Deb Pilutti (Simon & Schuster, 2018)

The Dinosaur's Diary
by Julia Donaldson (Puffin, 2007)

The Word Collector
by Peter H. Reynolds (Orchard Books, 2018)

Word Wizard series
by Robin Johnson (Crabtree Publishing, 2015)